D0569654

The Private Realm of

MARIE
ANTOINETTE

The Private Realm of

MARIE ANTOINETTE

MARIE-FRANCE BOYER

PHOTOGRAPHS BY FRANÇOIS HALARD

WITH 123 ILLUSTRATIONS,
108 IN COLOUR AND 15 IN DUOTONE

THAMES AND HUDSON

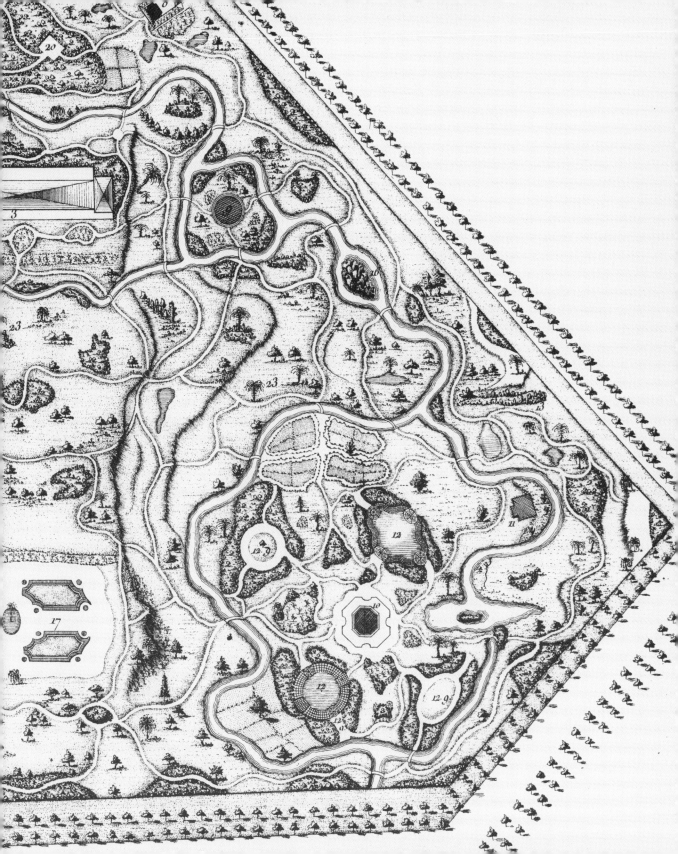

FOR MIN HOGG,
WITHOUT WHOM THIS BOOK
WOULD NOT EXIST
M.-F. B. & F. H.

DESIGNED BY MICHAEL TIGHE

Translated from the French by Jenifer Wakelyn

Marie-France Boyer has been responsible for the research, text
and concept of this book, but wishes to thank François Halard for his
creative contribution in the visual field.

First published in France in 1995 as *Les Lieux de la reine Marie-Antoinette*
© 1995 Thames and Hudson Ltd, London, and Thames & Hudson SARL Paris
English translation © 1996 Thames and Hudson Ltd, London
Photographs © 1995 François Halard (except those listed on page 112)

British Library Cataloguing-in-Publication Data
A catalogue record for this book is available from the British Library
ISBN 0-500-01690-9

Printed and bound in Great Britain by Jarrold Book Printing

Frontispiece: the mirror alcove in the Méridienne.
Pages 4–15: detail of a layette casket celebrating the birth of the
Dauphin; mother-of-pearl encrusted secrétaire by Riesener in
the boudoir at Fontainebleau; a garden design for the Trianon; a blue
armchair by J.-B. Sené; detail of the great canopy, or tester, of
the ceremonial bed in the queen's bedchamber at Versailles; fragment
of a toile de Jouy lambrequin; a cottage in the Hameau.
Contents page: a sphinx from the decorations of the Salon Doré in the
Petits Appartements at Versailles; a detail of the boudoir at Fontainebleau;
an engraving by Lerouge; the statue of Almathea by Pierre Julien in the
Laiterie at Rambouillet; a detail of the gardens of the Hameau at Versailles.
Background, this page: Marie Antoinette, engraving by
L. J. Cathelin after F. Drouais.

CONTENTS

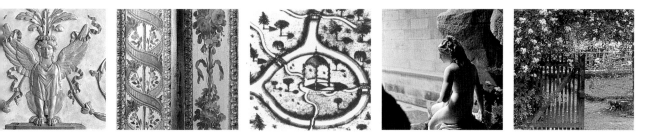

PREFACE

In 1774 Marie Antoinette became queen of France; in 1793 she went to the guillotine. For more than a decade, her position enabled her to commission the decor, furniture and objects that she delighted in, and to indulge her every whim. She became a great patron of the arts, and enjoyed all forms of frivolity in a supremely frivolous age. Was her taste her own, reflecting her personal preferences and her extravagance, or was it a unique expression of the spirit of a whole epoch? Her marriage brought her into the grandiose apartments and anterooms of the queens of France. Crowded at all hours with milling servants, traders, visitors and courtiers, these chambers were full of tiptoeing footsteps, abrupt collisions and pestilential odours, and the young queen could never reconcile herself to this atmosphere. Louis XVI gave her the Trianon: 'What a lovely dream was this palace with its magical garden,' wrote the Goncourt brothers, 'where at last she could take off her crown… escape from supervision… and from discipline,… and enjoy solitude and friendship, open her heart, relax, indulge herself and live.' Other retreats followed, each more intimate than the one before. The queen employed the same craftsmen to work on these alterations – Mique, Riesener, Jacob, Sené and Lagrenée, Boulard and the Rousseau brothers; 'She prefers to listen to those who give her the greatest pleasure,' was the wry comment of her brother, Emperor Joseph II of Austria. On her arrival in France the queen was already influenced by the taste of the Austrian court; she loved the seventeenth century, *pietre dure*, imposing bronzes, and anything oriental – like her mother, the Empress Maria Theresa, in this if in nothing else. Dazzled by Louis XV, she adopted his style. Did she help to develop the more austere style which goes under the name of her husband Louis XVI? Did she influence the virtuoso craftsmen who are unquestionably among the greatest produced by France? Did they follow the excesses of her frivolous imagination – or did she merely take up a fashion that had been invented by others? The elegant swing, the nocturnal revels of Fragonard's paintings, are perfect illustrations of the life which the queen desired to lead in her boudoirs and follies. In these pages we have tried to capture echoes of this fairy-tale existence and to evoke her taste and her imagination as they were expressed in the rooms, the furniture and the objects that she loved.

Marie Antoinette was born in Vienna in 1755, a daughter of the Habsburg Empress Maria Theresa of Austria. She was married to the Dauphin of France at the age of fifteen. Her childhood in Vienna and Schönbrunn was comfortable and happy; she sang, danced, made music and acted in plays with her brother and sisters – and gorged herself on cream choux pastries. She met the young Mozart, and helped him up when he fell full-length on the polished floor of the empress's chamber; he said, 'You are good, I would like to marry you.'

When Louis XV embarked on an alliance with Austria, the choice for marriage to the Dauphin fell on the twelve-year-old Antonia, who had still not learned to read. The empress adored her children and brought them up in great freedom. When the formal proposal came, she kept her daughter with her in the evenings to educate her,

INTRODUCTION

but it was too late. So, at the age of fourteen, Antonia left her warm and affectionate family life and set off alone with her little lapdog. She did not speak French, and her first notable achievement was to blot the marriage contract. Fortunately, Louis XV adored her. Her complexion was rosy, her walk graceful and her bearing aristocratic. The 59-year-old king, still gallant and handsome, delighted in the fresh charm of her youth and showered her with jewels. Next in line to the throne was his orphan grandson, a clumsy sixteen-year-old. The future Louis XVI wrote 'Nothing' in his diary for his wedding night, and went off hunting. Seven years and an operation would be necessary before the marriage could be consummated. Feelings of

guilt meant that the Dauphin could deny his Dauphine nothing. Strong as an ox, his own favourite pursuits were riding and shooting, and he had a passion for lock-making. The two became good friends. The future queen began her public life by refusing to submit to any form of constraint, ritual or etiquette, hiding in the servants' quarters and playing with their children. At Louis XV's funeral in 1774 she laughed behind her mourning fan, remarking on the dowdiness of the old princesses.

Two untalented and untrained adolescents had come to power; things were going badly for the country. Louis XVI was full of good will but it was not enough; his ministers, Turgot and Necker, failed to drive home urgently needed but unpopular reforms. France was hurtling to its ruin. In 1789 Louis XVI summoned an assembly of the States General. Although he was well-intentioned, flexible and always ready to negotiate, the king's life was to end in ruin. He was imprisoned and finally guillotined in 1793, dignified to the end but overtaken by the events of history.

As for Marie Antoinette, while happy to use her position to help her friends and even to place them in important posts, she nevertheless refused to play the part expected of her. In his famous biography Stefan Zweig explains: 'She was neither the great saint of royalism nor yet the great whore of the Revolution, but a mediocre, an average woman.' At the beginning of her reign, when she seemed to embody the hopes of all sides, she was acclaimed. Her long-enforced chastity doubtless explains in part her extreme frivolity, her heedlessness and her thoughtless extravagance. 'My daughter has little taste for serious application,' wrote Maria Theresa to her ambassador, 'moreover she is quite ignorant and she gives me much anxiety.' The young queen was surrounded by bad influences. Her first friend was the gentle and faithful Princesse de Lamballe (who was to have her head cut off by the mob because of this friendship), but later she fell under the spell of the Comtesse de Polignac. Witty, cynical and intelligent, the new favourite succeeded in establishing her own circle.

The queen was so happy with the 'Comtesse Jules' that she put her children in her charge. The two women were inseparable, and would go from the nursery to the theatre, spending the night dancing at masked balls, accompanied by the king's brother and a group of frivolous young men with whom they dallied until dawn. The queen played for huge sums at cards – even the forbidden faro – while apparently retaining her legendary virtue. Nevertheless, at the age of eighteen she fell in love with Axel de Fersen, a Swedish officer in the French army, who was to remain loyal to her all his life and who later served the royal family in tragic circumstances.

In 1778 she finally gave birth to her first child: Madame Royale, whom she nicknamed 'Mousseline la sérieuse'. She had four children, two of whom survived her. The maternal role was important to her, and gave her a degree of maturity. But she had already overstepped the mark: ten years after her accession, she was the subject of insulting verses, a byword for debauchery and financial ruin. Falsely accused of intriguing to purchase a priceless diamond necklace, she was implicated in a spectacular scandal of fraud and theft. Her friends abandoned her; the king, humiliated, was obliged to publish his accounts. The queen was nicknamed 'Madame Déficit'. After this everything happened very quickly. Three years later the mob invaded Versailles calling for her head. The royal family escaped, but was recaptured and brought under escort to Paris. Imprisoned first in the Tuileries and later in the Temple and the Conciergerie, the royal couple would never see Versailles or enjoy freedom again. 'Tribulation makes one realize what one is,' declared Maria Theresa's daughter, an exemplary prisoner who went to her death with great dignity. 'Destiny will at times transform a mediocre human being…. In the last hour of her life,' wrote Stefan Zweig, 'Marie Antoinette became tragic and finally achieved a greatness commensurate with her destiny.'

24

Portrait de Marie antoinette, Reine de France, d'essiné aux tuileries, par duplessi bertaux.

Anyone who joins the crowd that sweeps through the queen's bedchamber at Versailles every day will always hear one of the visitors exclaim, 'Well, I wouldn't want to sleep here!' Colossal, gilded, the vast state bedchamber consists almost entirely of a throne-like canopied bed with silk draperies that is indeed hardly conducive to sleep. It is out of scale because it is first and foremost an emblem of power; a bed made for a queen, not for a woman. Here the four children of Louis XVI came into the world to continue the dynastic line, here Marie Antoinette received the court and her official visitors. But, hating etiquette, she deserted this solemn arena as soon as she could, spending most of her time in the 'petits appartements', hidden behind her chamber with its enormous bed. Two doors on each side of the great tester, the bed-canopy, lead into a series of rooms the size of those we live in today, if

THE PETITS APPA

not smaller. The doors are concealed within the Grand Broché de la Reine, a brocade hanging of white silk embroidered with lilacs, peacock feathers and ribbons by Philippe de la Salle, a craftsman from Lyons who also worked for the Tsar of Russia. Under Louis XIV and Louis XV the apartments that were to be taken over by Marie Antoinette were used as service rooms; they opened on to a dark interior courtyard often disturbed by the shouts and drinking bouts of the guards. They occupied three floors: on the top floor, right under the roof and away from it all, was a billiard room, full of natural light. Stairs led below to the apartments of the Enfants de France and their governess. Following the progressive and controversial principles of Jean-Jacques Rousseau, the queen wanted to keep her children near her. A low-ceilinged corridor used by the water-carriers led to the king's apartments. According to the custom of the time it was hung with draperies of white Berry cloth; these were changed frequently for hygienic reasons. The queen went to and fro *'en chemise'* in this labyrinth of little passageways; it would have been quite impossible to negotiate them in the towering coiffures and the vast panniers that adorned the formal dresses of the court ladies. These small rooms with their concealed doors

EMENTS

escaped the surveillance of spies and favoured love affairs and intrigues. To step through the looking-glass, just as Marie Antoinette used to do, is an extraordinary experience. The four main rooms, the Méridienne, the two libraries, the Salon Doré, their boudoirs and their bathrooms provide a perfect image of eighteenth-century France as we imagine it today. Louis XVI gave the queen the Méridienne (a room for resting) in 1782, just after the birth of the heir to the throne. She turned to the architect Mique who was then finishing a fanciful grotto at the Trianon. The room

28

Page 27: a fashionable headdress in the age of Marie Antoinette: 'A young and pretty queen who is endowed with every charm has no need of all these follies,' wrote the Empress Maria Theresa to her daughter.
Right: the Méridienne, the small octagonal salon decorated in 1782 to celebrate the birth of the Dauphin.

Near the mirror alcove in the
Méridienne *(right)*, a little Japanese
lacquer dog *(below)*, decorated
with gold maki-e (Edo period,
early 18th century), sent by Maria
Theresa to her daughter.

Opposite: a carving of a favourite
dog decorates the arm of a chair.
Inset: a letter from the queen to her
mother, explaining that, according
to the custom in France, she and
the king have separate bedrooms.

was to be white, with panelling by the Rousseau brothers, picked out with delicate bronze reeds, ribbons, Austrian eagles, peacocks, symbols of love, and dolphins (alluding to the birth of the Dauphin) designed by Forestier. Opposite the window the queen devised a daybed in an alcove lined with mirrors; their uneven surface made her utter a premonitory shriek one day, when she thought she saw herself with her head cut off! For the draperies of this alcove she coveted a very special fabric that required long and complex weaving. It was never to be completed, and the simple blue textured silk with tassels and fringes (of which an exact replica was made in 1950) was merely a

Il y a bien longtemps que nous couchons séparés, je croyois que, ma chere maman, ne l'ignoroit pas, c'est un usage fort general icy, entre mary et femme

temporary expedient. Today the furnishings of the Méridienne combine chairs that once belonged to the Comte d'Artois, the king's brother, with others made for Marie Antoinette; the originals disappeared during the Revolution.

The queen and the count shared the same tastes and ways of life and the same friends; they became the closest of accomplices. In 1777 the Comte d'Artois had built the Bagatelle pavilion after a bet with the queen. It was unique; perfection itself. But, unlike her brother-in-law, the queen

was still easily influenced and sentimental, and without a strong sense of style. On a chair already overloaded with ribboned fasces, rose garlands and Austrian eagles, she insisted on having the heads of her favourite dogs carved on the arm-rests. Maria Theresa, who knew her daughter's tastes, would often send her objects of Chinese lacquer to remind her of the oriental tastes of Schönbrunn – Buddhas, boxes of every shape, fans, inkwells, lotus flowers, little dogs, hens and hearts. They enchanted the twenty-year-old queen, who also adored objects made of jasper and petrified wood. Anything new, anything striking was seized on as a relief from boredom. Conversation in the Petits Appartements was confined to worldly gossip and discussions of the latest piece at the theatre. 'The talk was always desultory and disjointed,'

was one visitor's report. Nevertheless the queen resolutely discouraged flirtation, preferring to discuss fashion and hair-styles. At this time the ladies of the court wore extraordinary constructions on their heads that were as remarkable for their inventiveness as for their size. On the death of Louis XV, forests of cypresses were the rage; these were followed by English gardens and ships in full sail. Marie Antoinette innocently sent her mother a picture of herself thus adorned. 'I do not see a queen of France but an actress,' replied the empress. The setting for this light-hearted life seems exquisite to us; two centuries later we respond to the intimate atmosphere evoked by these rooms. Still strongly under the influence of Louis XV, the Petits Appartements were created by exceptional craftsmen, working by appointment to the queen, and the proportions of the four main rooms strike us today as perfect. The two libraries are plain and severe. One, high-ceilinged, is apple-green, and the other, lower and darker, is blue. Unlike the Méridienne, which is still essentially rococo in spirit, they look forward to the rigour of the Empire style.

es 32–33: the emblem of the Sun King *(left)* above the mirror alcove in the Méridienne, where the door bolts *(right)* have been attributed to Louis XVI. *Left:* a view of the blue library, ...ing towards the Salon Doré and the bathroom *(see pages 44–45) Right:* a detail of a *trompe l'oeil* painting of books bearing the queen's arms on one of the doors in the green library. The high-ceilinged green library *(overleaf)* connects the Méridienne to the blue library.

Doubtless the frivolous young woman, to whom books were of little interest, allowed the craftsmen a freer hand for innovation here than elsewhere, but the sophisticated adjustable metal brackets that support the shelves can only be attributed to her. Her books are bound in red morocco stamped with three fleur-de-lis. The room is bathed in the light falling from the huge windows. Doors hidden by a *trompe l'oeil* painting of books lead into the bathrooms and to the Salon Doré.

In the eighteenth century there was a profusion of fanciful, curvaceous furniture; one shape metamorphosed into another as pieces were moved from room to room, taking on a new function in each new location. So the queen would often have her hip-bath-on-wheels pushed close to a fireplace in the bathroom, or would even have her bed made up in there because it was warm. In winter she would sit in the tiny camomile boudoir adjoining the Salon Doré while the latest fashionable book was read to her (perhaps a play by the subversive Beaumarchais in whose work she had so unwisely appeared in the private theatre at the Trianon in 1785). A pair of upholstered chairs, *bergères* or *voyeuses*, moved close to the marble fireplace, was enough to furnish this 'corridor' measuring six by one and a half metres. The rocaille pastoral décor created in 1750 on the theme of shepherds and shepherdesses seemed old-fashioned to the queen and she decided to have it whitewashed. But she loved the room itself because it was on the way to her children's apartments. She could gossip there with the 'Comtesse Jules', Madame de Tourzel (her children's governess) or Madame Royale.

Another habituée was her dressmaker, Rose Bertin, who ruled supreme over this little world. In 1782 the queen ordered ninety-three costumes. She favoured lavender-blue chiné and fabrics patterned like marble or foliage, shades of lilac (sometimes with a white spot), white gros de Tours. The Petits Appartements were also the scene of frequent visits, perhaps nocturnal, from her faithful knight, Axel de Fersen. The Salon Doré was decorated later, around 1783–84, and is in a different style and on a different scale. Less original than the other rooms, it has a separate entrance. With its Pompeian-style bronzes, symmetrical mirrors, sophisticated furniture and pompous gilding, it is at once private and public. Here Marie Antoinette received her official guests in a more formal manner. Her servants wore a red and silver livery. Because of the disturbances caused by the guards, she obtained a new suite in 1788 that gave on to a better-placed courtyard on the ground floor. Here Mique designed a bathroom in bluish-grey, the walls adorned with stucco decorations on the theme of

Page 38: Marie Antoinette's emblem, three fleur-de-lis, embroidered on her gaming-purse. *Page 39:* the queen's seal (bronze by Lorthior, enamel by Cotteaux).

Right: the Salon Doré, decorated in 1783 by the Rousseau brothers. It opens on to the camomile boudoir, which the queen had whitewashed. *Above:* detail, after restoration.

water. To prevent damage from the heating system, some of the panels were carved in stone. These motifs interweave an exquisitely delicate gossamer pattern of fountains, dolphins, lobsters, swans, shells and white corals, representing the Louis XVI style at its most perfect. After taking her bath behind a two-way mirror, the queen liked to be massaged on a high daybed in this beautiful, light room.

She scarcely had time to enjoy this new creation. On 5 October 1789, less than a year after it was completed, a page in the queen's scarlet livery came to fetch her from the Trianon. Through an opening in the grotto, as she rested on a mossy bed, she saw him running towards her. 'Paris is marching on Versailles,' he said: these few words made her hasten back to the château.

She showed no sign of nervousness in the evening, when she gathered a few friends together in the Salon Doré. 'I know that they are coming for my head,' she declared, 'but I have learned from my mother not to fear death and I await it with resolution.' She had long been preparing herself for this moment. That night the guards of the château were massacred, and a mob baying for the queen's heart had already entered the ceremonial chamber when she fled through the secret corridors to the king's apartments. The clock in her chamber meanwhile continued to sing out its childish refrain: 'It's raining, it's raining, shepherdess; gather in your white sheep….'

Throughout her life, Marie Antoinette loved neo-classical decorative motifs inspired by Herculaneum and Pompeii. The bronze winged sphinxes, perfume burners, arabesques, festoons, serpents and cupids of the Salon Doré were created by the Rousseau brothers, who also worked extensively for the Comte d'Artois.

The blue decoration of the great bathroom was designed by Mique and was not completed until 1788.

Today it houses a daybed made for Louis XVI in 1785 by Boulard, who also designed the steps.

As conceived by Mique and the Rousseau brothers, the theme of water in the great bathroom encompassed shells, lobsters, tridents and waterfalls as well as [sw]ans, dolphins, fossils and corals.

'You love flowers, Madame; and so I have a bouquet to give you.' Legend has it that with these words Louis XVI made his wife the gift of the Petit Trianon. She began by spending the afternoons there, returning to Versailles in the evening. But after the birth of Madame Royale, an outbreak of measles gave her an excuse to stay the night. She liked it so much that she decided to spend more time there, and the architect Mique was asked to undertake some alterations. He was to become a faithful interpreter of the queen's desires. The Petit Trianon had been

THE PETIT TRIANON

designed by Ange-Jacques Gabriel as a pleasure house for Louis XV and Madame de Pompadour, was used by the king and Madame du Barry, and it was from this retreat that Louis XV was carried to his deathbed in the Château of Versailles.

The Petit Trianon is considered by many to be 'one of the most beautiful buildings in the world' (Cyril Connolly, *Pavilions*, 1962). According to the Comte de Fels, it was 'the most perfect masterpiece of the decorative arts of the eighteenth century'. In his view, 'Marie Antoinette brought to it only her own decadent taste.' Her alterations, however, were few: a banister was added to the great staircase, and she had white muslin hung over the sea-green panelling of the Cabinet du Roi (the Trianon was never grey, as has been claimed: the darkening of the white paintwork of later years has given rise to this myth). The furniture was covered in crimson

Pages 48 and 49: a design for an elegant swing, and a tree; engravings by Lerouge, 1784. *Below and right:* the pavilion designed by Gabriel for Louis XV in

the garden of the Petit Trianon, ten years before Marie Antoinette commissioned the building nearby of the temple of Love and the Belvedere pavilion.

silk trimmed with gold, and a bed as narrow as that of a convent schoolgirl was installed (this is not surprising since the conjugal bedroom was not the custom in France). The king only came to the Trianon when invited, and never slept there; sometimes the guests would move the clocks forward to make him leave earlier. In the rest of the building the young Rousseau brothers who worked with Mique fashioned the Pompeian-style stucco decorations that the queen loved. These were genuine stylistic innovations, although the Comte de Fels dismissed them as 'pale copies'.

The stamp of Marie Antoinette's personal taste, always inspired by the miniature, is more evident in the pleasure houses in the park which she planned with Mique: the Temple of Love, copied from that of the Sybil in Tivoli, and, above all, the Belvedere.

Here, guarded by six sphinxes, the octagonal interior boasted a ceiling painting by Lagrenée and walls decorated with sculptures of garden tools and emblems of love by Le Riche. The gold and white furniture was covered in the queen's favourite blue gros de Tours. This charming building was to become one of her most costly projects.

She also had a theatre built on the site of Louis XV's orangery; the greenhouses and the rare species in his model zoo bored the queen almost as much as the disheartening straightness of Le Nôtre's gardens. At first her fancy was for a Chinese garden, but she chose the English style with little meandering streams and paths, and 'natural' hills, rocks and grottoes, which, in fact, were endlessly designed and redesigned.

The pleasure house built for Louis XV, once the realm of gallantry and flirtation, thus became the setting for a comfortable, bourgeois way of life. The queen lived there much as today we might live in a country house of seven or eight rooms. She received Axel de Fersen and her close friends there, the unscrupulous Polignacs, the Comte d'Artois as well as Esterhazy and Vaudreuil – 'all that is worst and youngest in Paris', commented Maria Theresa. On Sundays she even received visits from children and their governesses, refusing in this way to follow the dictates of her rank.

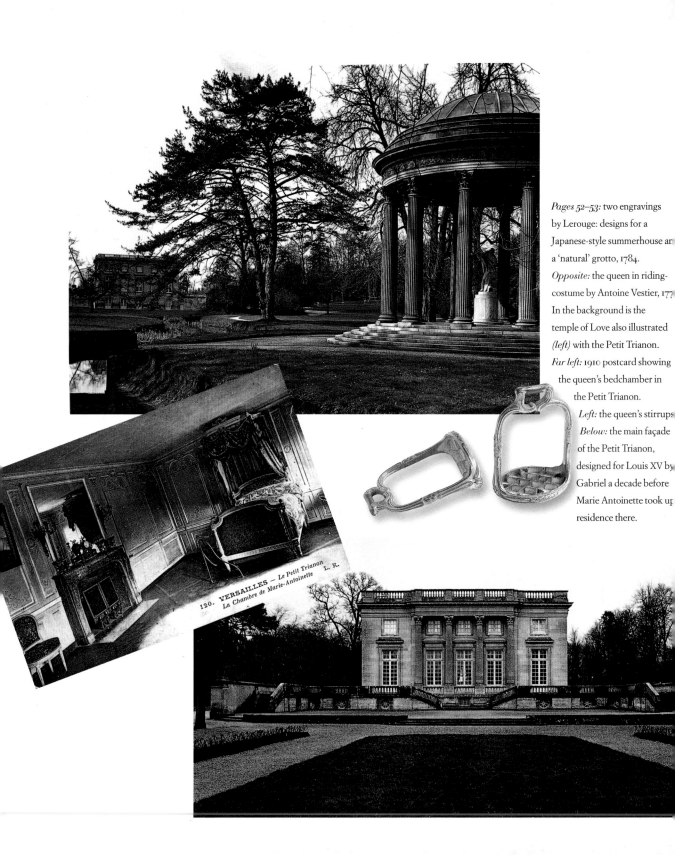

Pages 52–53: two engravings by Lerouge: designs for a Japanese-style summerhouse ar a 'natural' grotto, 1784.
Opposite: the queen in riding-costume by Antoine Vestier, 177
In the background is the temple of Love also illustrated *(left)* with the Petit Trianon.
Far left: 1910 postcard showing the queen's bedchamber in the Petit Trianon.
Left: the queen's stirrups
Below: the main façade of the Petit Trianon, designed for Louis XV by Gabriel a decade before Marie Antoinette took up residence there.

120. VERSAILLES — Le Petit Trianon L. R.
La Chambre de Marie-Antoinette

The old nobility were anathema to her: Rohan, Orléans, Noailles, all were kept at a distance. Idle and resentful, deprived of their sovereign and of the etiquette essential to their very existence, the courtiers began to desert Versailles. Meanwhile the queen amused herself by giving magnificent night parties that might have been inspired by the paintings of Watteau. Lamps were hung in bushes, statues and pleasure houses were lit up by burning torches, while here and there her accomplices were hidden, disguised as fauns or shepherds. On one occasion she persuaded her friends to dress up as shopkeepers, pastrycooks and chocolate-makers in little stalls linked by garlands of flowers and leafy bowers. To receive 'the Norths', as she called the grand duke and duchess of Russia, she laid on a sumptuous festival which began in the theatre. In her hair the grand duchess wore a jewelled bird mounted on a spring

above a rose made of rubies. The queen was sick with envy; the French fashion of slipping a flat bottle full of water below a headdress of fresh flowers was eclipsed. But always impulsively generous, she made her guest a gift of her own fan which had a diamond lorgnette set in the handle. 'The Norths' were enchanted. In the daytime they played on see-saws and at games of blind man's buff, and imposed bets and ambiguous forfeits on each other. In the evenings they played cards with passionate absorption; after a visit to his sister, Joseph II expressed anxiety over this gaming-house atmosphere. The little world of the Trianon adored the drama. Frequent rehearsals were held in the blue and gold theatre with its moiré hangings and scenery painted to look like marble. Unused to such rites under Louis XV, the court was shocked, but the royal family, most importantly the king himself, were happy to be spectators. The queen recalled the playlets she enacted with her brother at Schönbrunn. It all seems quite innocent; but in the world outside it was whispered that the 'Austrian whore' plastered her room with diamonds that should have been used to feed the people. Aware of the rising tide of these calumnies, the Austrian ambassador spoke sternly to the queen. 'What do you want me to do?' she replied, 'I am terrified of being bored.'

The queen commissioned Mique
to build the Belvedere pavilion,
reflected *(right)* in the water.

Opposite: a view of the interior.
Above: a bronze key for
the Petit Trianon.

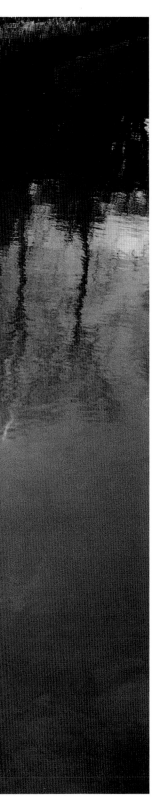

It was in just such a grotto as this
(engraving by Lerouge, 1784)
that the queen was resting at the
Trianon on 5 October 1789,
when she had to hasten back to the
Château of Versailles.

A few years after settling into the Trianon in 1783, Marie Antoinette decided to build a hamlet nearby. The idea itself was not new: the Prince de Condé had one at Chantilly, and there was another at Méréville. Jean-Jacques Rousseau was all the rage, and the village ambience was extolled by painters such as Greuze, Le Nain and Chardin. Mique set to work, assisted by Hubert Robert; the project was to take four or five years. Countless canalizations drew off enough water from Marly to create a lake which became the centre of the whole village, consisting of a farmhouse, a mill, a barn, the queen's house, her boudoir, a guards' cottage, a gardener's cottage, a tower, a dairy, a dovecot and a henhouse. To set the desired tone of humble poverty, the painters Tolède and Dardignac decorated the dozen little houses with imitation cracks, splits and false half-timbering, and

THE HAMEAU

carved mossy stones and rotten wood that bring to mind Snow White and the Seven Dwarfs. The queen insisted on real animals to show to her children – cows named Brunette and Blanchette, ducks, goats, sheep, and a billygoat from Switzerland, 'good-tempered and very handsome'. The flowers she loved were planted in pots, decorated with her emblem, from the Saint-Clément factory. The houses were swathed in honeysuckle, Virginia creeper and hollyhocks. Madame Vigée-Lebrun often painted her holding a bloom like the Fantin-Latour rose, the 'painter's rose'. The queen liked to wear the thin cotton dresses that scandalized the court; she was accused of going out in her chemise. Heedless, she would go thus attired to watch her strawberries and cherries being picked, to see corn being ground, laundry washed,

and cows milked (after they had been brushed and cleaned for her visit). She drank her milk from Sèvres porcelain, and would lead her lambs into the fields on ribbons.

Inside, little remains of this rustic veneer. The Hameau, it is said, once contained rooms decorated with lattice-work and furnished with chairs and tables made from reeds and branches, and draped with starched muslins and toiles. The queen's love of printed cottons – particularly those designed by Oberkampf at Jouy – was a sore point with the silk manufacturers of Lyons, as the queen's taste had set a whole new fashion. A liking for simple materials did not, however, prevent her from commissioning the furniture for the billiard room, the Chinese salon and the neo-classical salon from Riesener and Jacob, the official craftsmen of Versailles. Only close friends, indeed, were welcomed at the Hameau – but these happened to include the queen's brother Joseph II, the Tsarevich, and Gustavus III of Sweden, travelling incognito. This false simplicity did not deceive everyone; the Prince de Ligne found the queen 'trop ruban' – too fussy and frivolous.

In 1785 the Hameau was still incomplete when Marie Antoinette was implicated in the Affair of the Diamond Necklace. Today, at the far end of the park of Versailles, the Hameau is still charming despite its melancholy air. It is more like a painting by Hubert Robert than a real country village. And every year among the visitors to this sweet-scented idyll there are those who claim to have seen the queen's white-garbed ghost flit by.

Pages 62 and 68–69: watercolour designs by Chambé for exteriors, plans and sections of the 'cottages' in the Hameau, 1782. *Below:* postcards of 1910.

Left: behind its rustic façade, the queen's house boasted a dining room, a gaming room, a billiard room, a library, an antechamber and a private apartment.

posite: Elisabeth Vigée-Lebrun painted Marie Antoinette twice in the same year (1782): holding a rose, and *'en gaulle'* – in the thin muslin dress she used to wear at the Hameau and which scandalized the court.

73

Designed by Mique between
1783 and 1787, the mill, the dairy,
fairy-tale 'cottages' and the
Marlborough tower *(far right)*, w
decorated with climbing plants, a
seventeen hundred and thirty-tw
glazed pots from the Saint-Cléme
factory, all with the queen's embl

The mill: jasmine, roses, myrtles
and rudbeckias embellished the

external walls, which were artistically
painted with imitation cracks.

Marie Antoinette did not like hunting. Having to remove to the king's beloved Château of Fontainebleau every autumn was intolerable. This tradition dated from the eleventh century, and the vast edifice bore witness to its long ancestry both in its architecture and in its interiors. Set in a forest full of game, the château was completely isolated, at least a day's coach journey from Paris, but the entire court would migrate there. Louis XVI and Marie Antoinette had eight state apartments and there the etiquette of Versailles was recreated. There were 172 apartments for the courtiers, but many more had to find quarters in the town. Their names were written in chalk on the doors of their rooms, in yellow if they were princes.

On two sides of the state bedroom of the queens of France – where Marie Antoinette never slept – she created two rooms that she particularly treasured. The Salon de Jeu

THE BOUDOIR AT F

or gaming room, was in neo-classical style, and later used by the Empress Josephine; its furniture is now sometimes displayed in an Empire-style setting. Behind the tester of the great bed (which was as large as the room it concealed), the queen concocted a tiny boudoir so perfect that none of her successors dared to make any alterations (although Marie Antoinette would have loved the swan-necked bath installed by the Empress Eugénie). Perhaps the most attractive room left to us by the queen, this boudoir has an atmosphere of fantasy and fable. She coveted a gold and silver boudoir on the theme of the iridescent pearl. More personal and private than the Salon de Jeu, this boudoir was created in 1786 by the same craftsmen: Barthélémy, Rousseau and Roland. The *voyeuses*, conversation chairs, and *ployants*, folding chairs, in the gaming room were by Séné and Vallois; the furniture in the boudoir was the work of Riesener and Jacob. As in the Méridienne, some of the door and window fastenings have been attributed to the locksmith's art of Louis XVI himself.

By now the queen had forfeited her popularity, but her husband was more indulgent than ever; she had just given him a second son. The Duc de Normandie, the future Louis XVII, was just one year old when his mother commissioned from Riesener the steel, bronze and mother-of-pearl furniture which, like her porcelain breast cups (see page 93), survive as magical reminders of her imagination

TAINEBLEAU

and caprice. The mother-of-pearl furniture is probably unique. The Moghul technique of studding furniture with mother-of-pearl in a fish-scale pattern had inspired German cabinetmakers, but the results had never been so accomplished or so stylish. Born in Germany, Jean-Henri Riesener had an extraordinary career. He was apprenticed at the age of twenty to Oeben, the famous cabinetmaker to Louis XV, and he was still working under the Consulate. When Oeben died, Riesener married his widow and took on his client list. He was employed by Louis XVI from 1774 onwards, and became famous for the *bureau à cylindre*, the roll-top desk, that he made for the king, as well as many commodes and secrétaires. In 1784, he stopped working for the Mobilier National (the furniture of the royal household), when the king was obliged to economize. Marie Antoinette took this opportunity to become his most important client. When he created the furniture for the boudoir he was fifty years old and his art was at its zenith. We cannot say who first conceived the idea of using mother-of-pearl. We will never know whether it was at his suggestion that, from a thousand unrealizable desires, she chose the one that he could fulfil, or whether he set out to captivate a patron who was always avid for the new. Whatever its original inspiration, the legendary secrétaire is the consummate expression of Riesener's refinement and craftsmanship, and marks the transition from the baroque spirit of Louis XV rococo to the purer lines of Louis XVI style. Always austere, if not severe, Riesener's designs do not eschew ornament. The pearl motif, a network of matt steel bands making diamond-shaped frames for the inset mother-of-pearl, highlights each edge and corner of the secrétaire. With the little matching sewing table, it forms a quite exceptional ensemble, which disappeared during the Revolution and was only returned to Fontainebleau after its amazing rediscovery in 1961. More conventionally, Riesener often set medallions of Sèvres porcelain and Chinese lacquer into marquetry

Page 79: a detail of the decoration of the boudoir at Fontainebleau. *Page 81:* a detail of the secrétaire by Riesener; rectangular bronze plaques depict plump cherubs, the same age as the Duc de Normandie, in the guises of the arts of Painting and Architecture. *Right:* a cherub's foot escapes from a sculpture by Philippe Laurent Roland representing the Muses (one of the nine is missing) which embellish the overdoors *(opposite)* – the chair is by Jacob. *Far right:* one of the queen's beloved little dogs, painted by an unknown eighteenth-century artist.

designs of floral motifs in rare woods. These more formal pieces are fascinating for their virtuoso skill, but they strike the modern eye as relatively unadventurous.

Light spills from the mother-of-pearl to the framed mirrors which surround the room, and bathes the matt gold panels that complement the pearly sheen of the silver paintwork. These panels combine Pompeian motifs with the garlands of flowers that were famous for their 'simplicity'. Naturally, they included rose buds, but also, more unusually, daisies, cornflowers and ears of corn entwined with ribbons and garlands. Like the feet of the Jacob chairs and the mother-of-pearl furniture, the gold panelling repeats the theme of iridescence festooned with ribbons.

A dawn sky painted by Barthélémy floats above the high reliefs portraying the Muses, carved in plaster by Roland. The magical effect of these materials and their consummate craftsmanship must be completed in our imagination by the vision of voluminous, rustling taffeta, satin or gros de Tours dresses of white, blue or lilac. The reflections of two or three such apparitions in the glimmering light of the candelabra were enough to give an atmosphere of secret festivity to this little room, from which the sound of whispers and carefree laughter would spill out into the adjoining corridors.

Pages 84-85: as in the Méridienne, some of the ironwork in the boudoir at Fontainebleau may have been made by Louis XVI. *Opposite:* a porcelain cup celebrating the birth of the Dauphin; in the detail *(above)* the figure of his sister can be seen in the background. *Below:* a general view of the boudoir, created on the theme of the pearl in 1786 by Barthélémy, the Rousseau brothers and Roland; the original furniture by Jacob and Riesener has survived. *Top right, and this page:* details of the polychrome decoration.

The polychrome decoration of
the boudoir: intertwining flowers
and ribbons reminiscent of
contemporary silks manufactured
in Lyons. The vertical motifs and
stripes are characteristic features
of the Louis XVI style.
Overleaf: the queen used many
variants on the intertwined
M and *A* of her initials, painted
here by the Rousseau brothers.

In June 1787 Louis XVI delighted the queen, whose childish and impetuous character he knew so well, with a surprise gift: this was the Laiterie at Rambouillet. He took his wife to the end of the park to look at two small symmetrical towers; between them hung a curtain of branches. At a signal from the king, the curtain of foliage dropped to reveal the dairy, which he had planned in great secrecy with the architect Thévenin.

The two little pavilions were surrounded by rare trees; inside, the salons were decorated with grisailles on the theme of the four seasons painted by Sauvage. The painter Hubert Robert had designed a remarkable set of chairs in archaic style, made by Jacob. Etruscan in inspiration, these mahogany chairs combined motifs from Herculaneum with Egyptian palmettes and rams' heads. They were covered with a

THE LAITERIE
at Rambouillet

cloth of nasturtium orange, braided with black, an idea that Marie Antoinette found 'picturesque'. These little-known chairs, which have had an eventful history, recently returned to France and can be seen in Versailles once more. They have nothing in common with the furniture of Oeben and Sené, but look forward to the the nineteenth century – as does the architectural style of the exterior of the Laiterie. A few steps lead up to the main entrance, flanked by two columns and set beneath a pediment embellished with a marble medallion of a cow suckling her calf signed by the sculptor Pierre Julien. This is a temple dedicated to milk. The façade, built in blocks of ivory-coloured sandstone, has a force and an austerity reminiscent of the architecture of Ledoux, whose Saltworks at Arc-et-Senans was built ten years earlier.

93

The king had his own reasons for encouraging the queen's extravagance. As a change from Fontainebleau, he liked to hunt at Rambouillet; it was too far to return to Versailles every night, and so in 1783 he had bought the estate from the Duc de Penthièvre. The queen liked this new domain even less than Fontainebleau; to her it was a charmless 'desert', an 'odious' residence, a 'toad-hole'. The king, however, wanted her company, and had built for her a model farm with three hundred and thirty-five merino sheep. But this was not enough to interest Marie Antoinette. At the Prince de Condé's estate at Chantilly, and on the estates of the Duc d'Orléans at Raincy, Louis XVI had seen the fanciful dairies that were now the height of fashion. He knew that the queen adored Mique's dairy in the Hameau at Versailles, and decided that it would be surpassed. He chose a site near a charming cottage encrusted with shells – a little house fit for Hansel and Gretel. This was also the work of

Thévenin and Hubert Robert, commissioned in 1779 by the Duc de Penthièvre for his granddaughter, the Duchesse de Lamballe, the queen's great friend.

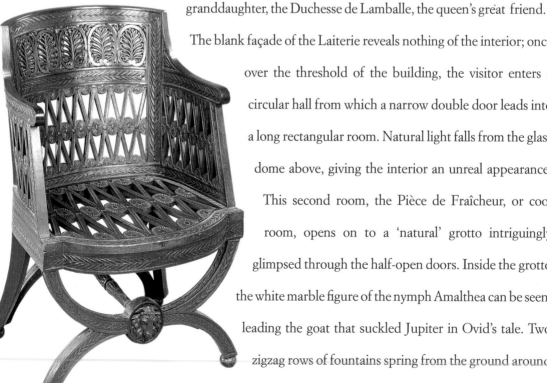

The blank façade of the Laiterie reveals nothing of the interior; once over the threshold of the building, the visitor enters a circular hall from which a narrow double door leads into a long rectangular room. Natural light falls from the glass dome above, giving the interior an unreal appearance. This second room, the Pièce de Fraîcheur, or cool room, opens on to a 'natural' grotto intriguingly glimpsed through the half-open doors. Inside the grotto the white marble figure of the nymph Amalthea can be seen, leading the goat that suckled Jupiter in Ovid's tale. Two zigzag rows of fountains spring from the ground around

Page 93: a Lagrenée breast cup
in polychrome Sèvres porcelain,
and a design for a cheese-strainer.
These objects were intended to
fill the niches and consoles in the
antechamber to the Laiterie.
(*pages 94–95 and right*). To please
the Empress Marie-Louise,
Napoleon replaced the white

marble floor designed by Thévenin
with a rose-des-vents compass
design, incorporating an imposing
Empire-style table at the centre.
Above: the statue of the nymph
Amalthea in the grotto at the
end of the second room can be
glimpsed from outside.
Opposite: a mahogany chair by
Jacob for the Laiterie.

Right: the Pièce de Fraîcheur is lit by natural light from above and ends in a grotto. Fountains on each side cooled the milk-pails; designs for these had been chosen by the queen from the selection painted in watercolour *(opposite)* by Lagrenée, which are also shown in more detail *(pages 98–99 and 102)*. Although a number of the imitation-wood pails were made, many of the other designs were never produced.

the entrance to the grotto, where classical vases filled with milk were placed to cool. For these two rooms, Pierre Julien designed a series of neo-classical medallions and marble bas-reliefs placed at mid-height. Rural imagery, drawing on antique motifs, celebrated the pastoral mood of a refined and decadent aristocracy who advocated a return to nature. Gods mingled with shepherdesses; nymphs went about their down-to-earth tasks of butter-making or sheep-clipping in an atmosphere of amorous intrigue. The relief depicting Jupiter raised by the priests of Cybele was followed by Mercury stealing the flock of Admetus. These sculptures have long since disappeared. The Empress Josephine, whose taste was impeccable, had them placed at Malmaison, where she too had a dairy. Today the stone walls of the Laiterie are bare, the niches empty.

As remarkable and memorable as the building itself, which was inspired by the ideas of Jean-Jacques Rousseau, were the furnishings and above all the china which was specially designed for the dairy. Probably commissioned by Hubert Robert from the designer Lagrenée to be made in hard-paste porcelain at Sèvres, these pieces were intended to embellish tables and niches and to provide rhythmic accents on the black and white floor in the Pièce de Fraîcheur. A few have survived, as has a tabulated set of drawings in watercolour showing

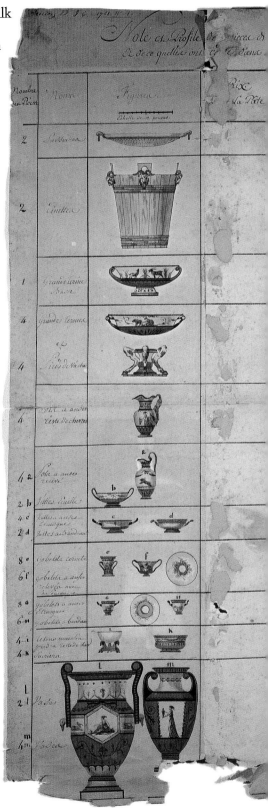

the designs selected for production. Even the Wedgwood china made for the dairy of the Duc d'Orléans at Raincy cannot vie with the unbridled extravagance of these polychrome creations. Jars with goats' heads, vases with Etruscan handles, terrines with cows' legs, horned sugar bowls and goblets, buckets made of imitation wood in the Niderviller-style; full rein was given to an extraordinary abundance of invention.

Even more astonishing are the breast cups. These, mounted on tripods with goats' feet, were rumoured to have been moulded from the queen's own breast. Etruscan tints clothed these porcelains: Pompeian red, violet, purple, brown, ochre or khaki (not  white or gold as in the reproductions made later for the Empress Marie Louise, Josephine's successor). Did Marie Antoinette actually use this service – 'those precious useless objects,' as one critic of the day wrote, 'whose selection allows us to display our taste and wit?' The first half of the service was delivered in 1787; for two summers she may have drunk milk with her children and friends as they rested after playing their games. Pierre Julien did not complete the statue of Amalthea until 1788; the queen had little time left to enjoy the last gift bestowed on her by her ever-compliant husband.

Pierre Julien's white
marble nymph was not
finished until 1788.
Marie Antoinette had
little time to enjoy it.

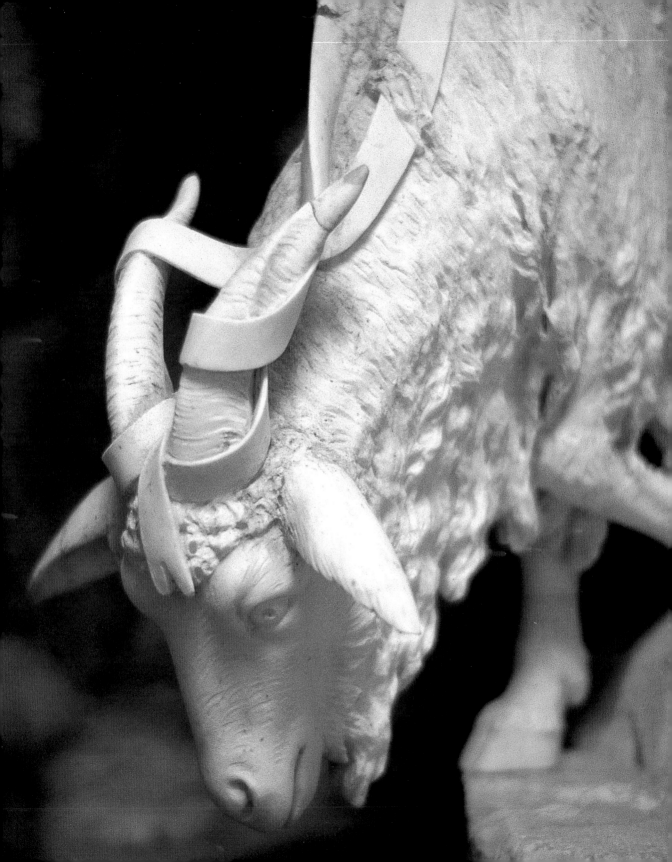

On 5 October 1789 the mob invaded the Château of Versailles. The queen fled through the network of secret passageways; for the time being, she was safe. But she and the whole royal family were taken under escort to Paris. In the Tuileries the next day she had the presence of mind to have some valued objects hidden away. They have survived until now as reminders of her taste. Crystal, porphyry, jasper set in bronze, and small anecdotal lacquer pieces characterize the sentimental taste of the daughter of Maria Theresa at the outset of her reign. At the other extreme, her last completed commission, the boudoir at Fontainebleau, bears witness to a markedly developed sensibility. The room decoration in Louis XVI style is extremely accomplished although not innovative – there are many similarities with the Turkish boudoirs created by the same artists in 1770 for the Comte d'Artois.

CONCLUSION

While the hamlets, pleasure houses, grottoes, the conversation chairs and writing desks were not the products of Marie Antoinette's own imagination, she did inspire the pastoral and mythological scenes of her favourite toile de Jouy. She left behind her, like Cinderella's slipper, objects that were as fantastic as they were unique. No trace remains of the diamond candelabra, the ivory and gold billiard cues or the fans set with jewelled telescopes, but we can still wonder at the mother-of-pearl secrétaire, the breast cups and the chairs with carved dogs' heads.

Some writers have castigated her love of the rare and unusual. 'The enthusiasm of a Parisian actress rather than that of a resident of Versailles' is the verdict of some art historians; 'characteristic of a young country-bred Austrian girl rather than a thirty-year-old queen of France'. For others, however, she represented a sublime embodiment, the perfect symbol of an *ancien régime* sensibility that has vanished for ever.

Two centuries later, the devotion felt by some of the French for this queen is shown by a cup, a scrap of fabric, a shoe or a medallion that has been miraculously saved and is now reverently displayed in an obscure château or in some prestigious collection. Now, after the passage of time, it is not always possible to assess the authenticity of these relics which have been so faithfully and fervently preserved.

Marie Antoinette was a fairy-tale queen who, in the harsh world of reality, died under the blade of the guillotine. Her favourite places still hold the ghost of her presence.

Page 106: there is a hidden door in the silk hanging designed by Philippe de la Salle for the queen's bedchamber at Versailles. Through this the queen escaped, and fled down the corridors of the Petits Appartements. As a prisoner in the Temple, she gave a miniature gold lyre *(opposite, top right)* and an unusual amber medallion *(page 107)* holding a fossilized spider, to her children's governess, Madame de Tourzel, who left it to her descendants.

Opposite, left: faience with the design called 'Mourning for the Queen', thought to contain a hidden portrait of Marie Antoinette. Like the blue china comfit-box *(opposite, below)*, it was made in the nineteenth century in her memory.

Left: on her way to the scaffold, 16 October 1793, the queen was sketched by David from his window. She was 38.

109

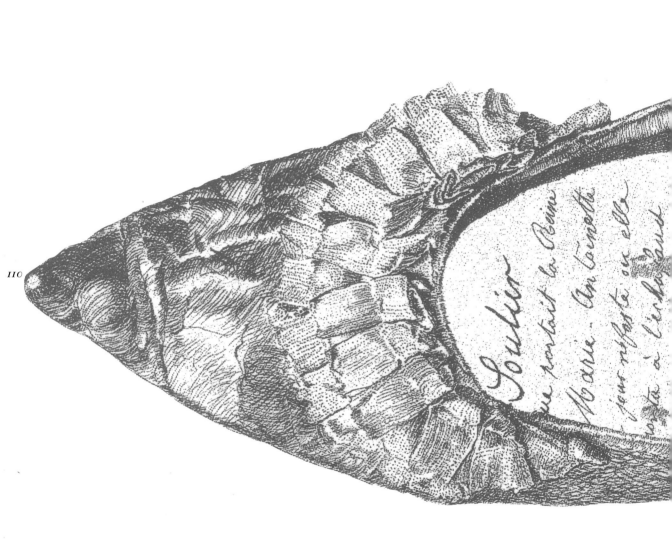

110

Above: the shoe said to have been lost by Marie Antoinette on her way to the scaffold. Engraving by Pierre Courtois, 1

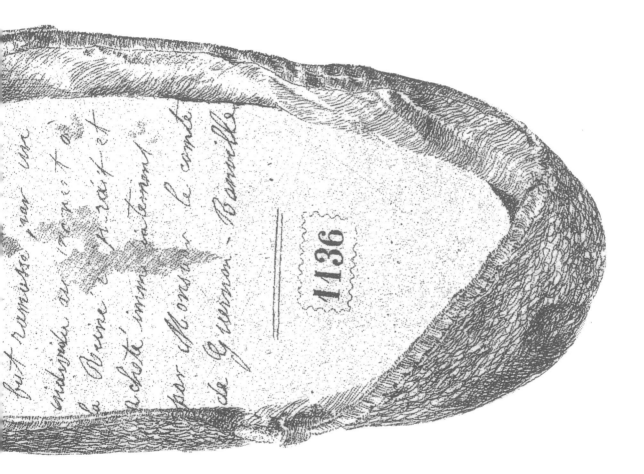

112: a design for a swing in an Anglo-Chinese garden,
~~~ving~~~ by Lerouge, 1784.

THE AUTHORS WISH TO THANK

FRANÇOISE DE NOBÈLE

LA BARONNE ÉLIE DE ROTHSCHILD

JEAN-PIERRE BABELON

CHRISTIAN BAULEZ

ROLAND BEAUFRE

LAURENT DE COMMINES

ISABELLE GRUFFAZ

PIERRE PASSEBON

DAPHNÉ DE SAINT-SAUVEUR

GOGO SCHIAPARELLI

BARBARA WIRTH

LE MUSÉE DE CAEN

THE WORLD OF
INTERIORS

Photographic Credits:
Musée d'art et d'histoire de la ville de Genève. Dépôt de la Fondation Gottfried Keller, page 21;
Giraudon, pages 62, 68, 69; Lauros-Giraudon, pages 66, 72;
Manufacture Nationale de Sèvres, Archives, Photo Jean-Loup Charmet, pages 93 (right), 98, 99, 101, 102;
©Photo RMN, pages 10, 27, 80, 93 (left), 96, 109.
Private Collections:
pages 1, 3, 8, 9, 12, 13, 17 (engraving), 18, 20, 25, 38, 39, 48, 49, 52, 53, 54 (postcard and stirrups),
55, 56, 57, 58 (key), 60, 61, 71, 83 (inset), 86 (cup), 88–89 (fabric), 107, 108, 110.

The quotations from Stefan Zweig are taken from *Marie Antoinette*, translated from the German
by Cedar and Eden Paul, Cassell: London, 1988.